THE ILLUSTRATED BOOK OF MONEY MANAGEMENT

Tanu Rishi, CFA

PREFACE

Why did Mike Tyson, MC Hammer, Nicolas Cage, Antione Walker, and numerous others earn millions and lose it all? Why do 70% of wealthy families end up parting with their wealth by the second generation? Why can 38% of Americans not come up with $500 without selling something or taking on debt? For the very simple reason that most of us are not prepared to manage money. Which begs the question - why are we not?

The idea to create the content of this book was born out of frustration that, no matter how educated my friends or I were (think of MBAs, Doctors, Accountants, PhDs), we made critical personal finance mistakes that cost us a pretty penny. It was evident that even though we were all highly literate, we were barely financially literate.

It is outrageous that something so fundamental to sustained success and mental well-being gets so little attention from the education system. How can algebra and the periodic tables be required curriculum while we are left to learn financial literacy on our own? I would be happy to trade my dismal performance on both those subjects for my financial literacy knowledge, for I know now the pitfall of not knowing sooner.

I hope that the content of this book will provide the core life skill of learning how to manage your money. I am confident that as these lessons have continued to help me on my journey to financial wellness, they will be equally valuable to you too.

This book is not another 'get rich quick' book, and I do not guarantee such a thing (as no one can). However, if you follow the fundamental principles, it will ensure that you don't end up poor.

"A formal education will make you a living; self-education will make you a fortune."

JIM ROHN

Abc
E=mc²
!!!
123
@
f(x)

CONTENTS

TAXES
20
20

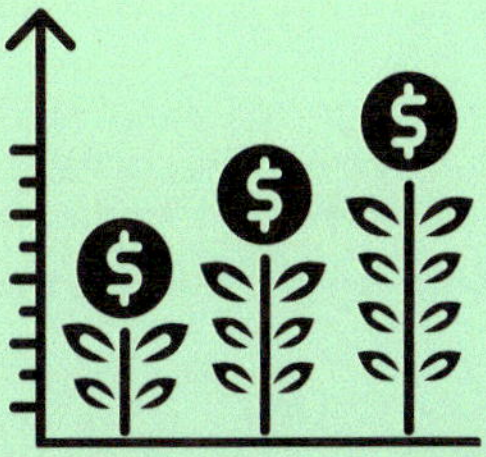

Dedicated to my maternal grandfather - Uday Dvivedi, whose wisdom I carry, and who taught me that the best use of knowledge is to share it.

To my parents whose unrelenting support made this small-town girl, against all odds, a successful New Yorker.

To my sister and my dear friend Toni, without whose acute observations, this book would have been completed in half the time.

Lastly, to my teacher and mentor, Prof. Kingshuk Mukherjee. He has shown me the path to possibilities, where I thought none could exist.

Let's begin the journey with eight basic financial literacy topics. We will be joined by Slick and Savv to enlighten us on the critical learnings.

1

KNOW YOUR PAYCHECK

In this role play, Slick and Savv will discuss the following topics:

1. Gross pay and Net pay
2. Different components of a paycheck
3. Tax-free deduction and taxable amounts
4. Money you will actually end up with compared to your salary

Hey Slick! I got that part time job at the space shuttle company
OMG! Doing what?
Umm.. concierge attendant
Stop sulking, you are still studying. They are not going to make you the CEO

Maybe that will inspire you to be an engineer
Or an Astronaut
You should be happy you'd be making your own money

Wow! I am already dreaming about making all that money

I will be making a $1,000 a month.

No you won't. I can show you why not.
$250 X 4 weeks = $1,000. I am great at math!

Here is why you won't get to keep the entire $1,000. Look at the table that breaks down your salary. Red is what gets deducted and green is what you will ultimately get as your final salary

Salary Break Down

	Gross Pay	This is your salary for the month	$1,000
Minus	Insurance (Medical, Dental)	You need to buy insurance for medical needs	-$100
Minus	Retirement Plan (401k retirement fund)	This is money you save for old age	-$60
	Taxable Income	You pay tax on this amount	$840
Minus	Taxes	This is what you pay to government to build roads, keep police & army	-$126
Minus	Social Security (FICA) (6.2% of your income)	This is govt. required retirement fund	-$62
Minus	Medicare (FICA) (1.45% of your income)	This is govt. required medical coverage program	-$15
	Net Pay	This is the money you actually get in your pocket	$637

Your **Net Pay** is the money that you receive after taxes and other deductions.

Net Pay will always be less than your Gross Pay.

Plan your spending based on your net pay and not your gross pay.

As much as I am shocked, I am glad that I now understand how much money I will actually be getting. This will help me better plan for my spending. Thank you for a valuable lesson Slick!

You are welcome! You should never spend more than you earn.

Know Your Paycheck

QUIZ

1. Your gross pay is :

A. Pay before FICA contributions
B. Pay before paying any tax
C. All of the above

2. FICA contributions include :

A. Social security only
B. Medicare only
C. Social security and medicare

3. Fedral and State taxes are incurred on :

A. Your net pay
B. Your gross pay after deduction
C. Neither- taxes are for dummies

4. Which of the following are tax-free deduction from your paycheck ?

A. 401k Retierment plan and insurance payments
B. 401k Retierment plan and alimony payments
C. Insurance payments and alimony payments

5. Your net pay is :

A. Pay after all deductions
B. All before tax money
C. Total amount of money that your employer pays you

1.C | 2.C | 3.B | 4.B | 5.A

2

WHAT IS BUDGETING?

In this role play, Slick and Savv will discuss the following topics:

1. Understand the concept of budgeting
2. Different categories of a budget and what they represent
3. Money allocation to different categories

Look Slick! My first ever paycheck.
That's wonderful! I am so proud of you
o you know what
ou are going to
do with the money
Hmm.. I am not sure
You can create a budget.

What is a Budget ?

Budget is the process to clearly define how will you use your money. Budgeting is a plan that helps you stay disciplined about saving and spending

A Budget can be divided into **four** primary categories

The first category, or bucket, is that of income. Income bucket is your **NET** pay that you use to distribute to the other categories.

Budgeting - Plan of allocating your money and sticking to it!

Income Bucket

- In hand salary/Net Pay
- Tips

Second, and most important, is the **Savings** bucket. This is the bucket you must put your money in before you plan for any spending. The amount can be as small or as big as your can afford

Income Bucket

- In hand salary
- Tips

Savings Bucket

- Rainy day
- Pay your future self
- (investments)

The third bucket is the **Needs** bucket. This is your everyday essentials and paying your bills bucket.

- Rent
- Food
- Utilities
- Transportation (Car Payments, Gas, Insurance etc.)
- Debt Payments (Students Loan)

The Fourth bucket is the **Wants** bucket. This bucket is for your recreation, entertainment and splurging.

- Recreation
- Entertainment
- Fancy Toys
- Exotic Travel
- Private jets
- Yacht
- Second , third , Fourth house

A good budget will follow the guideline to allocate Net Pay as below:

- **20%** to the saving bucket
- **50%** to the needs bucket, and
- **30%** to wants bucket.

Wants are unlimited, so be mindful to not transfer your saving to this category. It can be a slippery slope!

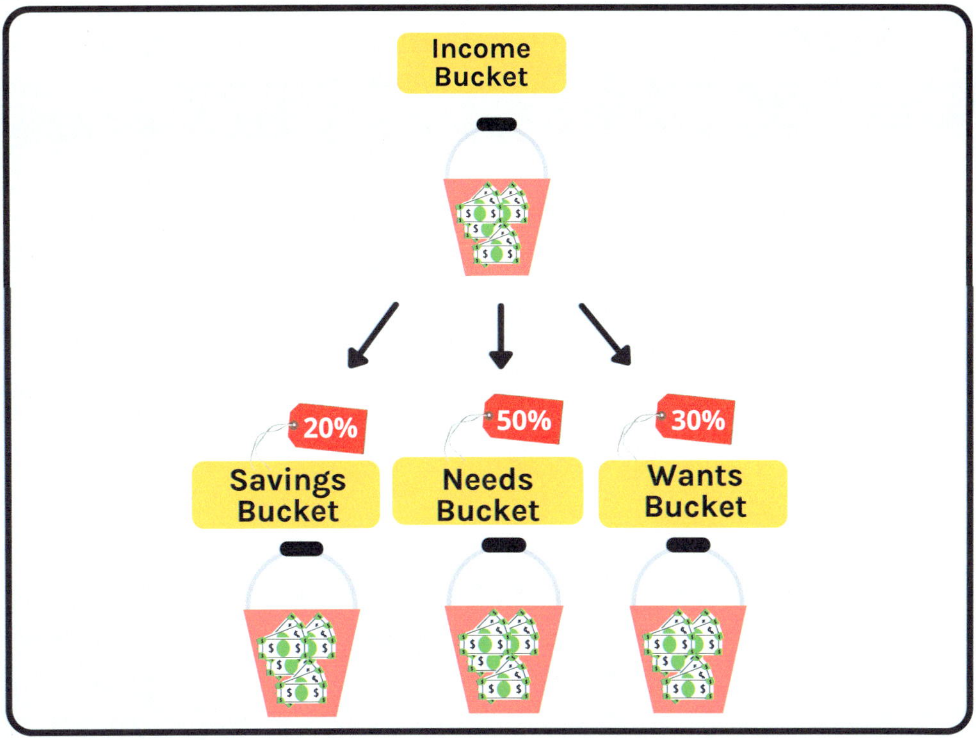

Are there any good apps for budgeting ?

There are plenty. Go ahead and find yourself one to get started. Remember , budgeting doesn't have to be perfect - it is a tool to provide you guidance. Just make sure you try to stick to it as much as you can. Happy Budgeting !

What Is Budgeting

QUIZ

1. Following is not one of the budgeting bucket :

A. Saving bucket
B. Income bucket
C. tax bucket

2. How much income should you allocate to the WANTS bucket ?

A. 50%
B. 30%
C. 60%

3. How much income should you allocate to the NEEDS bucket ?

A. 50%
B. 10%
C. 25%

4. For budgeting to be effective, which of the following behaviour is most important ?

A. Being disciplined about spending per the defined allocation
B. Being happy you made a budget
C. Being lazy to periodically check your spending

5. A budget is :

A. Fixed for life
B. flexible and should be adjusted for changing circumstances
C. For fun and has no real use

1.C | 2.B | 3.A | 4.A | 5.B

3

WHY BANK?

In this role play, Slick and Savv will discuss the following topics:

1. Why do we need to bank and different advantages of banking
2. The process to open a bank account
3. Different services that come with a bank account

Hey ! Did you spend all the money you earned from your job ?

Haha !! didn't put my money in the piggy bank . I deposit it in the bank

What if the bank gets robbed ?
What if the house gets robbed ?
Come Slick ! Let me teach you a little banking today .
Why Bank?

The first reason you bank is for **safety**

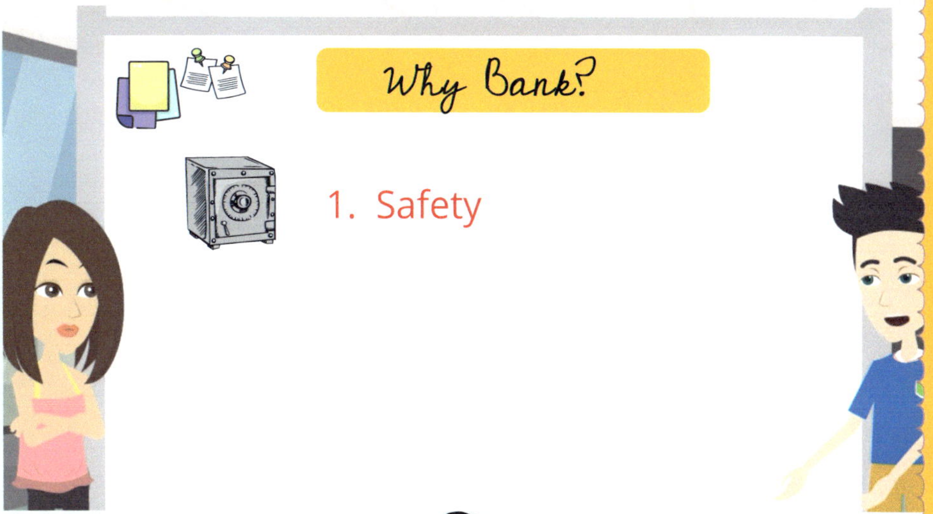

- If the robber robs the bank , your money will still be safe

- But if the robbers rob your home , your money is gone

Second, you bank for **convenience**

- With the availability of ATMs you have easy access to your cash

- You can also use checks or a debit card for all your purchases without carrying your cash around

Third, you bank for **security**

- In the US, the FDIC insures all deposits upto $250,000. Similarly each country has government bodies to protect consumers

- So in case the bank goes bankrupt the FDIC will pay for your lost money .

Lastly, you bank to create **relationship** with the bank which can come in very handy for your future needs

Like when you need money for business or to buy a home. Long time customers often get special offers or more favorable banking terms .

I want a bank account . how do I open one ?

Once you turn 18 , you need a few documents with which you can open one at any bank of your choice .
08:20

Walk into any bank's branch to open an account. You will need:

- Bank's form to provide your Name and address
- Your Social Security in the U.S or citizen's ID card that your country issues
- You may also need your passport or any government issued ID with a photo
- Some money to open the account with

Each country has its own identification ID, so you can use that instead of the Social Security number. For example, India uses an Adhar card and Europe uses European Social Security Number (ESSN)

Banking can really make life easy and offers many great services. Below are the "**cool**" parts of the banking

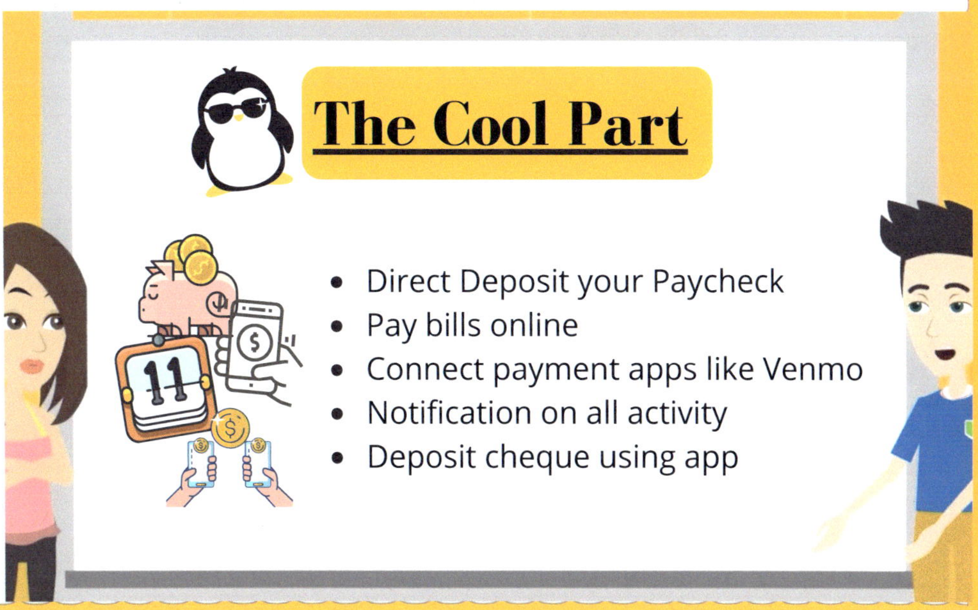

- Direct deposit saves you the hassle of depositing checks and sometimes the bank will pay you to set up direct deposits. Be sure to make use of that.

- You can enable notifications to keep track of all your account activity

- You can use your bank account to pay your bills including credit card bills, and link apps like Venmo for quick and free money transfers to your friends for the pizza they bought you the other day .

- You can even deposit checks without leaving your room by using an app. Most bank apps can do this now.

Banking can also result in unnecessary costs if you don't follow some basic rules. These costs are known as fees. Be mindful of these fees and charges as they can become significant very quickly. That is the '**uncool'** part about banking.

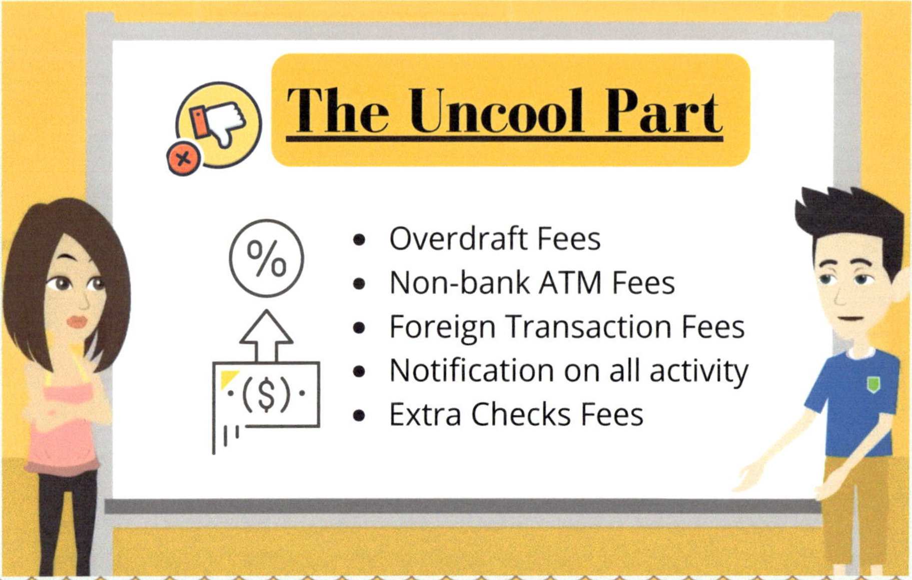

- **Overdraft fees** is charged when you don't have enough money in your account and you have a payment that comes due either via automatic payments or a check that you have written

- **Non-Bank ATM fees** is charged when you use an ATM other than your own bank

- **Foreign transaction fees** are charged when you use your debit/credit card when you make a purchase in currency outside your country

- **Check bounce fees** is sometimes charged in addition to the overdraft fee for the checks that cannot be cashed due to insufficient funds

- **Extra check fees** is charged when you order checks from the bank. Paying or scheduling online payments can reduce this cost

Ok Slick! You are now all ready to bank!

I am excited to open my bank account and use all the services offered by banks. But I am also glad you cautioned me all about the fees and costs.

Why Bank?

QUIZ

1. FDIC in the U.S. protects all bank deposits up to what amount?

A. $ 250,000
B. $ 25,000
C. $ 2,500

2. Following are the reasons for having a bank account EXCEPT

A. Convenience
B. Safety
C. Money laundering

3. You need the following to open a bank account except :

A. Proof of insurance
B. Government issued ID (e.g Passport)
C. Social security card

4. Which fee is charged if you use an ATM other than your banks ATM to withdraw money

A. Non-bank ATM fee
B. Withdrawal fee
C. Transaction fee

5. What fee is charged if you don't have enough money in your bank account and a payment is authorized :

A. Later payment fee
B. Overdraft fee
C. Extra checks fee

1.A | 2.C | 3.A | 4.A | 5.B

4

CREDIT EXPLAINED

In this role play, Slick and Savv will discuss the following topics:

1. The concept of Credit
2. Different types of credit and what it costs you
3. Understand if Credit is right for you

Hey Savv ! I am glad I ran into you. I want to buy something but my allowance won't cover for it . Could you lend me some money?
Sure, but how will you pay me back? You don't have a job.
Umm..May be when I have one in the future.
Hmm.. Should I charge you interest?
Interest? What is that?
Ok sister! You are not ready to borrow yet.

So the money you borrow is not free money. It creates an obligation for you to return what someone lent to you.

"Credit or Debt is the ability to borrow and a promise to pay it back"

There are **three** types of credit.

1

The first one is a **consumer installment loan** which is borrowing for a specific purpose.

Consumer Installment Loans

These loans have **fixed payments** and need to be paid within a **fixed time.** An example would be loans to buy a car.

Fixed payment

Fixed time

E.g. Car Loans

2

Next is the **Credit Card Loans**. These loans facilitate day to day purchases and is an ongoing type of borrowing.

Credit Card Loans

Payments depend on how much you spend monthly so the payment will be **ongoing.**

Payments are not fixed and will depend on your spending

Payment are ongoing

Do remember to make timely payments and try paying your balance in full

3

The last category of loan is **Home Loans**, also known as mortgage.

Home Loans or Mortgages

The payment of these loans will depend on if you borrowed a fixed rate or a floating rate loan. The time to return the money will depend on what you chose as the length of your mortgage.

There are multiple options available to a home buyer to choose the type interest rate they want to pay and the years they want to borrow for

"Let's talk about cost of credit now. The loans or credit are not free."

Debt is not free. You have to pay something to use the money. This is called the **cost of borrowing.**

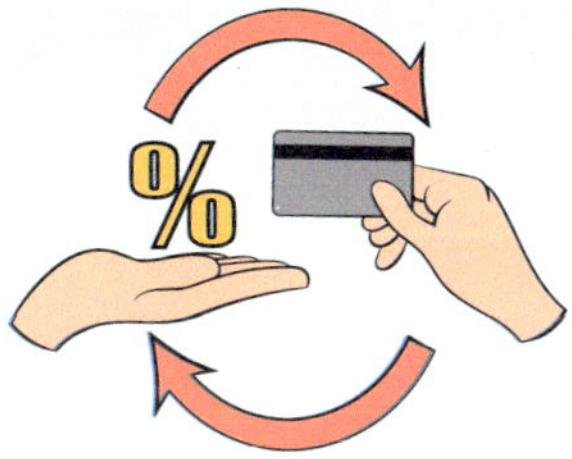

You pay:

1. Interest also known as Annual Percentage Rate (APR)
2. Fees

The financial institutions charge you this money because:

They are providing you the convenience of having the money when you need it.

They are also taking the risk that you may not pay the money back.

Whether you can borrow or not depends on two things :

1 . Your ability to pay back

- Either from the money from your job
- Or other sources of income

2 . Your intention to pay

- Intention means if you want to pay back the borrowed money
- Your credit score will reflect if you met your financial obligations as promised.

So in summary..

I have multiple options to borrow for my different needs..

..for which I have to pay interest..

..and if I don't pay back because either I don't have the money..

..or I just don't feel like it..

..it will ruin my credit score...

..which will then reduce my future ability to borrow...

Credit Explained

QUIZ

1. Buying a car on loan falls under which type of loan?

A. Equity loan
B. Consumer installment loan
C. Personal loan

2. Credit is typically not free. What do you have to pay to borrow?

A. Interest
B. Fees
C.Both 1 and 2

3. Your eligibility on how much you can borrow depends on which of the following?

A. How rich your parents are
B. How much money you will receive in inheritance
C. how much money you make and your credit score

4. A mortgage loan includes which type of loans

A. Home loan
B. Home equity loan
C. Both 1 and 2

5. Credit is :

A. Ability to borrow and promise to payback
B. Almost always free
C. Is always a bad idea

1.B | 2.C | 3.C | 4.C | 5.A

5

PROTECTING YOUR IDENTITY

In this role play, Slick and Savv will discuss the following topics:

1. Simple ways to protect your identity
2. The three credit bureaus and how to monitor your credit history for free
3. Understand the concept of Phishing and ways to protect yourself

Savv , remember how we were talking about credit the other day?
Yes
I found some really useful information online on how to protect our identities. It turns out, identity theft can greatly impact our credit rating which then impacts our entire personal finance ecosystem
Really? How worried should we be?
I think being aware and regular monitoring are good practices. Nothing to freak out about.
Tell me more!

Basics to Protect Identity

Say NO expensive credit monitoring services

Don't post any personal information online

Guard & destroy old personal information promptly

Set-up phone alerts for your cards

No need to sign up with expensive credit monitoring services. They charge you a ton of fees that are completely unnecessary. If you develop a little discipline to be watchful and follow some simple rules, there is no need to pay hefty fees to these companies.

Do not post your personal information like birthday and mother's maiden name on any website, social media, or otherwise. This includes posting your birthday without the year. We all love getting birthday wishes however it is not difficult for a hacker to guess your year of birth from the content of your social media account.

Follow some simple rules as below :

Don't writing your PIN on your cards or keep the pin in your wallet with your cards

Never carry your original government issued card (e.g. SSN); you rarely need it

Store all your financial paperworks securely and invest in a paper shredder

Set up alerts with your bank and credit card company so you know if someone used your account and you can act right away.

You can get your free credit report from each source once a year. Make it a habit to check each bureau's report every four months. This will keep you updated on any unusual activity a few times a year.

Additionally, you can freeze your account on each bureau, and only unfreeze your account when you need to. it might be a little cumbersome to freeze and unfreeze your account, but it is certainly an option.

Phishing is a fraudulent attempt to obtain sensitive information such as user names, passwords, and credit card details by disguising oneself as a trustworthy entity in an electronic communication.

The scammer disguises as a trustworthy company so you are tricked into giving the information.

Sometimes just clicking on links in the emails can expose a lot of your personal information without you actually providing it.

Always remember that the tax department, government agency or your financial institutions will NEVER ask for information using emails or over the phone. They always use post or ask you to come in the bank.

Don't click and take the bait !

What a productive weekend to learn all about protecting ourselves from identity theft!

We are ready to take on the scammers!!

Protecting Your Identity

QUIZ

1. All of the below are acceptable to post on Facebook EXCEPT :

A. Name of your school
B. The date you were born
C. your relationship status

2. The three credit bureaus are as below EXCEPT :

A. TransUnion
B. Experian
C. TransUrban

3. Phishing is :

A. Family outing to get some seafood
B. A slang word for fishing
C. Fraudulent way a scammer tries to get your personal information for financial gains

4. Which one is correct ;

A. It is OK to provide information if IRS calls
B. Click on the links in an email that says it is urgent or it will result in a big penalty from the IRS
C. IRS never calls, uses third party service or emails as a method of communication

5. Simple way to protect identity includes all EXCEPT :

A. Promptly destroy dated personal information
B. Set up alerts with your financial information
C. Write PIN on the back of your card , so you never forget

1.B | 2.C | 3.C | 4.C | 5.C

6

KNOW YOUR TAXES

In this role play, Slick and Savv will discuss the following topics:

1. What does progressive taxation mean
2. How are taxes calculated based on your income
3. Understand and calculate your 'effective' tax rate

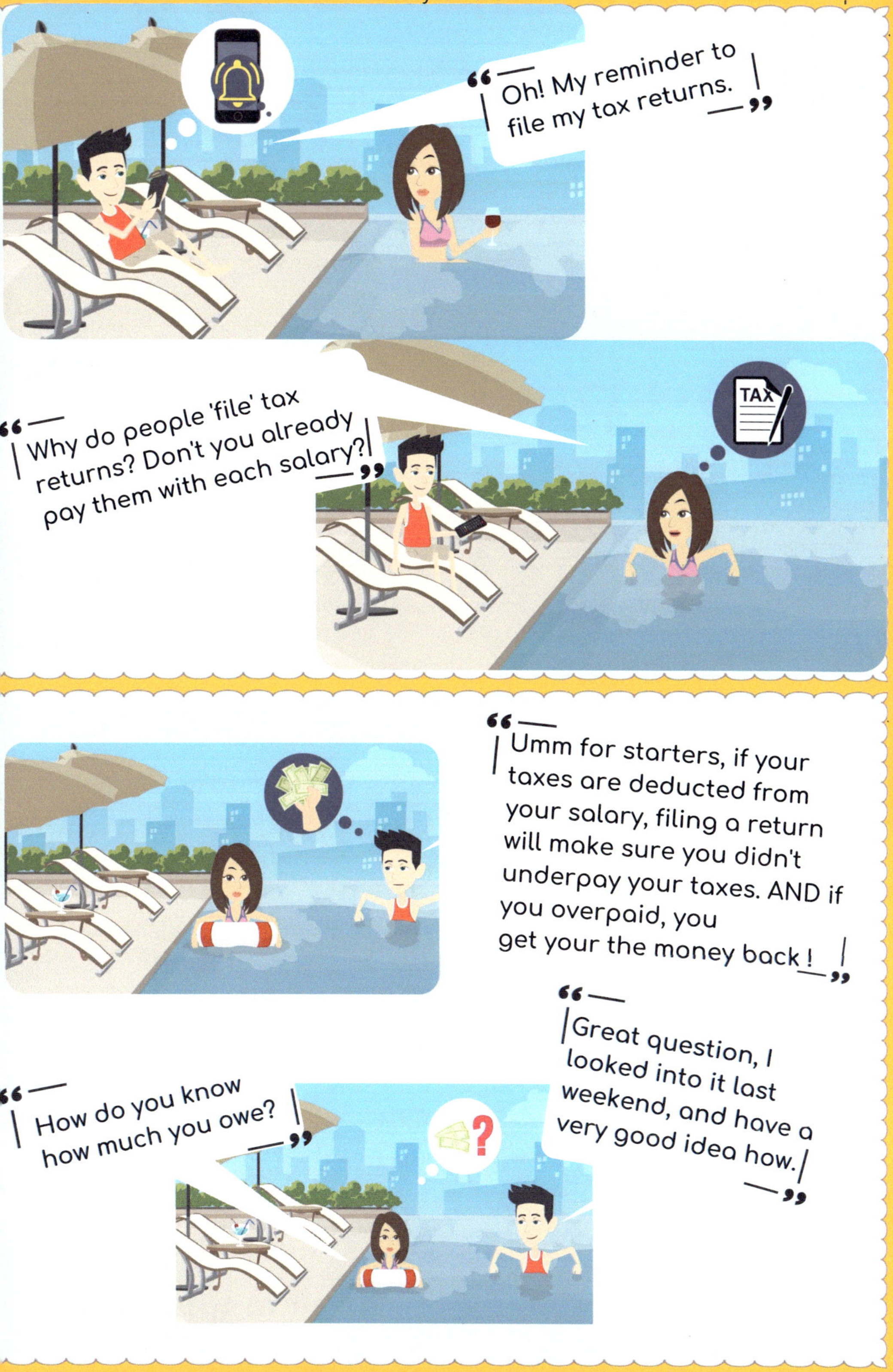
Oh! My reminder to file my tax returns.
TAX
Why do people 'file' tax returns? Don't you already pay them with each salary?
Umm for starters, if your taxes are deducted from your salary, filing a return will make sure you didn't underpay your taxes. AND if you overpaid, you get your the money back !
How do you know how much you owe?
Great question, I looked into it last weekend, and have a very good idea how.

Most countries use a progressive taxation system. This means, the tax rate, i.e. how much you pay in taxes, increases as your income goes up.

The tax rate progresses with progression of your income.

The table shows what tax rate is paid based on the money you make.

Tax rate	2020 Federal Tax Brackets	Simplified Brackets
10%	$0 – $9,700	**$9,700**
12%	$9,701 – $39,475	**$30,000**
22%	$39,476 – $84,200	**$45,000**
24%	$84,201 – $160,725	**$76,000**
32%	$160,726 – $204,100	**$43,000**
35%	$204,101 – $510,300	**$306,000**
37%	$510,301 or more	**$510,301 or more**

Based on the tax brackets in the table, you will only pay 10% on the first $9,700 then go on to pay 12% on the NEXT $30,000 of your taxable income.

When you subtract the upper and lower numbers you can get the "Next" level for each bracket. For simplicity, the buckets are also calculated in the table. These are rounded numbers to make understanding of the concept easy.

"So If I make $65k a year, I will pay 22%?"

"No, not with progressive taxation"

Taxes are calculated on your <u>taxable income</u> which is the amount that is left after taking out allowed deductions like insurance and retirement savings.

We already know from the lesson on paycheck that not all income is taxed.

Let's take an example. Say your total income is $65,000. There will be some money that you do not need to pay taxes on. Excluding that, you are now left with 'Taxable Income'.

Total Income	**$65,000**
Minus - Money that is not taxed (Deductions, retirement contribution, insurance etc.)	$15,000
Taxable Income	**$50,000**

Now let's start with $50,000 taxable income. Because your income is in the brackets, does not mean you will pay 22%. Let's look at the simplified brackets. Follow the steps to calculate your taxes.

Take your taxable income and start putting the money in the simplified bracket buckets. $9,700 goes in the first bucket, the next $30,000 goes in the next bucket and the remaining $10,000 goes in the third bucket.

Tax rate	2020 Federal Tax Brackets	Simplified Brackets
10%	$0 – $9,700	**$9,700**
12%	$9,701 – $39,475	**$30,000**
22%	$39,476 – $84,200	**$45,000**
24%	$84,201 – $160,725	**$76,000**
32%	$160,726 – $204,100	**$43,000**
35%	$204,101 – $510,300	**$306,000**
37%	$510,301 or more	**$510,301 or more**

Since there is no money left after this, it will be your last bucket. If however, you were making a lot more money you will continue bucketing the money until you reach your last bracket.

Now you have your bucket set, go ahead and multiply the tax rates. For the first bucket, you pay 10%, so $970. Similarly, the taxes for the next bucket will be $3600 and the last bucket will come to $2,200.

If you total all the numbers , you get the total taxes you need to pay - in this case **$6,770**.

$9700 X 10% = $970

$30,000X 11% = $3600

$10,300X 22% = $2,200

$6,700

Note -Some numbers are rounded for simplicity

"I see, this is much less than simply taking 22% and multiplying by $50,000 taxable income which would be $11,000. So I am paying much less taxes with the progressive tax system."

"Brillant Slick! since we are at it. Let's calculate your effective tax rate - meaning the tax rate that you actually pay."

Take the total taxes and divide it by your taxable income. In this case, the effective tax is about 13.5%.

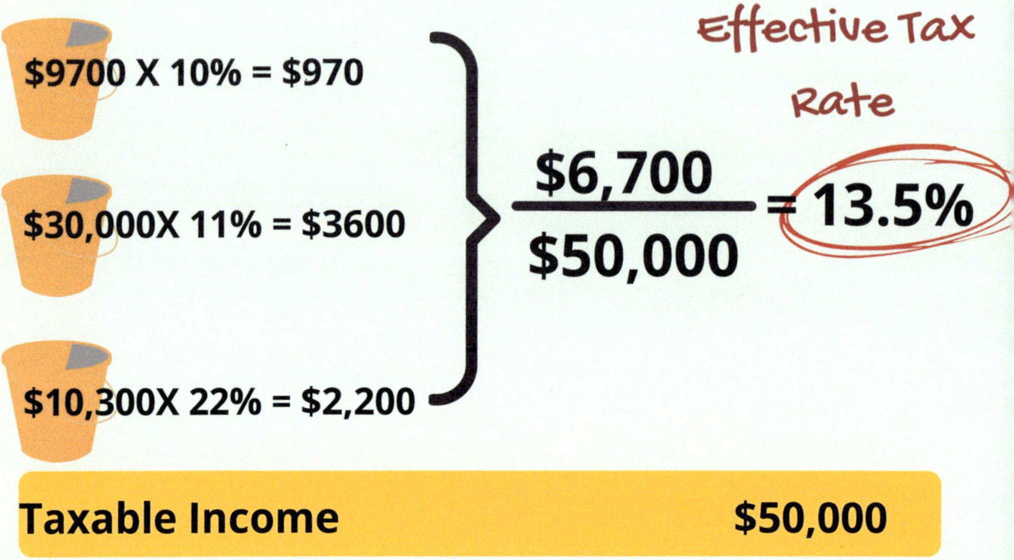

Know Your Taxes

QUIZ ?

1. What is a progressive tax rate system?

A. Pay progressively more tax every year
B. Make more money, pay more taxes
C. Taxes stay the same each year

2. What are tax brackets?

A. A tax rate table that represents % of taxes to be paid for the level of income you make
B. They are published guidelines by IRS for tax rates that will be applied to your income and are that is updated each year
C. Both 1 and 2

3. Taxes are calculated on :

A. Taxable income
B. Net income
C. Gross income

4. Effective tax rate is :

A. Tax rate for highest tax bracket
B.Tax rate calculated by dividing your tax by your taxable income
C. Tax rate that your parents pay on their income

5. Why is it important to file taxes on time?

A. To ensure you are paying necessary taxes as required by law
B. To correctly assess your tax liability and get money back if you overpaid
C. Both 1 and 2

1.B | 2.C | 3.A | 4.B | 5.C

7

WHAT IS INFLATION?

In this role play, Slick and Savv will discuss the following topics:

1. The concept of Inflation
2. Understand how higher prices are a result of Inflation
3. Understand how we can be protected from Inflation

Hey Savv meet my friend Rihanna.
What are you guys upto?
Inflation
We were reading about Inflation.

Interesting! Any fun learning to share?
Yes I would love to explain

Example
The concept is best explained with an example.

Say you wake up on a New Year's Day and make your way to your favorite coffee shop.

Let's assume that your coffee costs a dollar. You get served, you enjoy your cup, and leave saying thank you to the nice lady who served you your coffee.

On your return you find an exciting surprise from your grandma - $365 for a whole year of coffee at $1 a day!

Six months later .....

You continue your trips day after day thanking Grandma for such a lovely gift. Six months go by and then one day to your surprise, the coffee price has increased to a dollar **and ten cents.**

You quickly realize that Grandma's money is no longer enough to cover you for rest of the year. **This is inflation.**

The long term rise in the prices of goods and services caused by the devaluation of currency is **Inflation**.

Below are coffee prices over the years to show how inflation results in price increases.

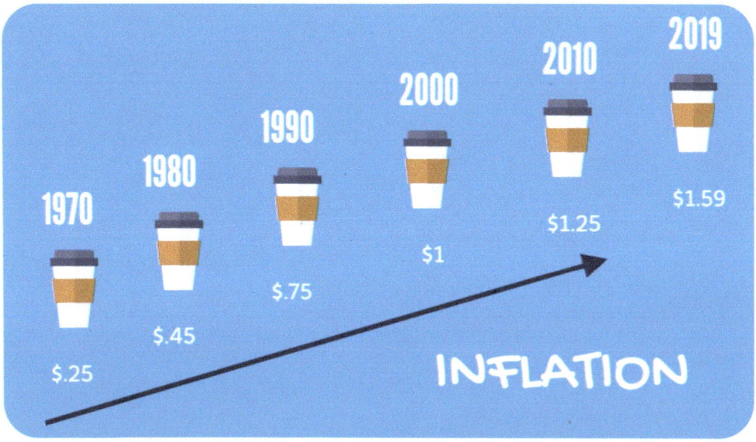

A movie ticket in 1976 costed $2.05; in 2019 it costs $9.16.

A Big Mac in 1976 costed $0.75 in 2019 it costs $3.99.

1 Increase the money you make

In your case ask grandma..
Ha Ha!

On a serious note, if you have a job, your employer should increase your pay at least at the rate of inflation.

and

2 Invest your savings

You should invest your savings after you set aside money for emergencies. This way when the price goes up due to inflation, your money grows too.

I think i have to run to my bank to take care of my savings !
Ha Ha !!
Ha Ha !!

What Is Inflation

QUIZ

1. What is inflation?

A. Long term price increase of goods and services caused by the devaluation of the currency
B. A concept for the rich people
C. When prices of goods and services remain the same over the long term

2. What was the price of Big Mac in 1976 vs 2019?

A. $ 2 in 1976 , $ 2 in 2019
B. $ 5 in 1976 , $ 2 in 2019
C. 75 cents in 1976, $ 3.99 in 2019

3. What are the options to protect your salary from inflation?

A. Ask your employer to increase your pay in line with inflation
B. Buy goods on credit cards
C. Both 1 and 2

4. When coffee prices go up over time it is due to :

A. Deflation
B. Inflation
C. More coffee shops opening in the neighborhood

5. What are the options to protect your savings from inflation?

A. Keep it in a bank account and do nothing
B. Invest your savings to earn at least as much as the inflaton
C. Both 1 and 2

1.A | 2.C | 3.A | 4.B | 5.B

8

COMPOUNDING EXPLAINED

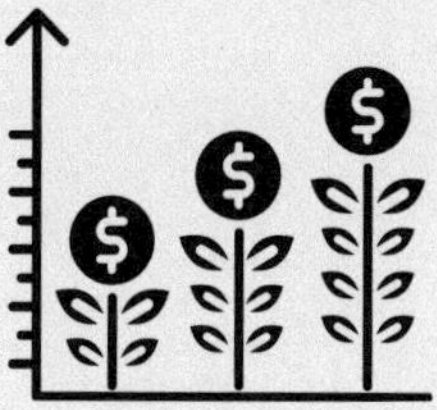

In this role play, Slick and Savv will discuss the following topics:

1. Concept of Compounding
2. How compounding helps money grow faster
3. How compounding is great for savings and very bad when it comes to debt

Let me start with defining what compound interest is. In very simple terms it is **interest earned on interest.**

Einstein once said :

"Compound interest is the 8th wonder of the world

He who understands it earns it, he who does not - pays it".

An example will be the best way to explain how compound interest works.

In our example we will:

- Invest **$1,000 for 5 years at 10% return** in two different scenarios
- In scenario 'A' we earn interest **only** on the principal of $1,000
- In scenario 'B' we will earn interest on principal **and** interest on interest.

	Year 1		Year 2		Year 3		Year 4		Year 5	
	Principal	Interest	Principal	Interest	Principal	Interest	Principal	Interest	Principal	Interest
Scenario A If you don't reinvest, you do not earn interest on interest	$1,000	$100	$1,000	$100	$1,000	$100	$1,000	$100	$1,000	$100
Scenario B If you reinvest and earn interest on interest	$1,000	$100	$1,100	$110	$1,210	$121	$1,331	$133	$1,464	$146
Extra Interest On Interest		$0		$10		$21		$33		$46

- At the end of Year 1, we will earn $100 on the $1,000 in both scenarios.

- In Year 2, scenario A invests the same $1,000 again, however, scenario B invests not only the original $1,000 but also the $100 interest earned from Year 1.Here is where the compound interest starts to show its magic.
- Notice how you will earn $100 in Year 2 for scenario A vs. $110 in scenario B. This is because you earned an additional $10 as **interest on interest.**
- Similarly, in Year 3 you earn the same $100 interest in scenario A, but $121 in scenario B. This is because you earned interest on interest from Year 1 AND Year 2.
- As more time goes by you make more money on the same $1,000 in scenario B when you let the interest compound.
- Just in 5 years, you make **$110 extra dollars which is 22% more** than if you were not letting the money compound.

Scenario A Total interest in 5 years = $100 + $100 + $100 + $100 + $100 = **$500**
Scenario B Total interest in 5 years = $100 + $110 + $121 + $133 + $146 = **$610**

Extra interest earned by compounding **$110**

1 Long term investments compound even more

"The longer the time period, the more the rate of growth"

The longer the time period, the more the rate of growth. If you apply the logic to **retirement** you will see that if you start investing early, you will need less money to achieve the same result compared to someone who starts investing in later years.

2 Higher Interest Rates Increase compounding impact

"The longer the time period, the more the rate of growth"

"Higher the growth of money"

The higher the interest rates, the higher the compounding amounts and thus even higher the growth of the money.

3 Compounding is not good when you have debt

"The longer the time period, the more the rate of growth"

"Higher the growth of money"

"You don't want loans that carry a high interest rate"

- The same principles apply when you take out loans. Hence you DON'T want loans that carry a high interest rate or loans that are for extended time periods (home loans can be an exception)
- Most importantly, it will be detrimental to your financial health if you take out loans that charge high interest rates AND are for longer time periods. You will make the lender a very rich person.

So be careful with credit card debts as they have very high-interest rates, try any pay in full each month, AND do not let the debt go unpaid for too long.
So there you have it - "Compound Interest" The 8th wonder!!
CREDIT CARD

Well, quoting Einstein again - I understand it, so I am going to earn it!
I guess I am ready for my assignment!

What Is Compounding

QUIZ

1. What is compounding?

A. An area in a building

B. Laying for something twice

C. When you earn interest on interest which results in your money growing faster

2. What is the effect of compounding on invested savings?

A. Savings grow faster

B. Savings grow slower

C. Compounding has no effect on how fast or slow the savings grow

3. How does compounding impact your retirement planning?

A. Early savings gives more time for your money to grow

B. Waiting to save for retirement will require you to put more money away later

C. Both answers are correct.

4. Which of the below is/are true for compounding?

A. Higher the interest rate, the higher the growth of investments

B. Longer the time period, the higher the growth of investments

C. Both answers are correct

5. What is the impact of compounding on loans?

A. If you don't pay off your loan, the interest from compounding makes a loan grow bigger

B. Compounding has no impact on loans

C. Compounding makes loans go away

1.C | 2.A | 3.C | 4.C | 5.A

Other content from the author

KNOW THE MARKETS

Learn about popular investment securities and how to invest:

1. Understanding Bonds
2. Understanding Stocks
3. Understanding Indexes
4. Understanding Risk vs. Return
5. Understanding Diversification
6. Make your First Trade

Order it on our website www.fiwe.app/the-book

DOWNLOAD THE FIWE APP

- Access all lessons as animated videos
- Available on Apple and Play store
- Register on www.fiwe.app with code FIWEFORALL to get free access to animations

CONTACT

@fiweapp

support@fiweapp

www.fiwe.app

Made in United States
Cleveland, OH
06 November 2026

47811156R00045

The United States Army War College

The United States Army War College educates and develops leaders for service at the strategic level while advancing knowledge in the global application of Landpower.

The purpose of the United States Army War College is to produce graduates who are skilled critical thinkers and complex problem solvers. Concurrently, it is our duty to the U.S. Army to also act as a "think factory" for commanders and civilian leaders at the strategic level worldwide and routinely engage in discourse and debate concerning the role of ground forces in achieving national security objectives.

The Strategic Studies Institute publishes national security and strategic research and analysis to influence policy debate and bridge the gap between military and academia.

The Center for Strategic Leadership and Development contributes to the education of world class senior leaders, develops expert knowledge, and provides solutions to strategic Army issues affecting the national security community.

The Peacekeeping and Stability Operations Institute provides subject matter expertise, technical review, and writing expertise to agencies that develop stability operations concepts and doctrines.

U.S. Army War College
SLDR
Senior Leader Development and Resiliency

The Senior Leader Development and Resiliency program supports the United States Army War College's lines of effort to educate strategic leaders and provide well-being education and support by developing self-awareness through leader feedback and leader resiliency.

The School of Strategic Landpower develops strategic leaders by providing a strong foundation of wisdom grounded in mastery of the profession of arms, and by serving as a crucible for educating future leaders in the analysis, evaluation, and refinement of professional expertise in war, strategy, operations, national security, resource management, and responsible command.

The U.S. Army Heritage and Education Center acquires, conserves, and exhibits historical materials for use to support the U.S. Army, educate an international audience, and honor Soldiers—past and present.

STRATEGIC STUDIES INSTITUTE

The Strategic Studies Institute (SSI) is part of the U.S. Army War College and is the strategic-level study agent for issues related to national security and military strategy with emphasis on geostrategic analysis.

The mission of SSI is to use independent analysis to conduct strategic studies that develop policy recommendations on:

- Strategy, planning, and policy for joint and combined employment of military forces;
- Regional strategic appraisals;
- The nature of land warfare;
- Matters affecting the Army's future;
- The concepts, philosophy, and theory of strategy; and,
- Other issues of importance to the leadership of the Army.

Studies produced by civilian and military analysts concern topics having strategic implications for the Army, the Department of Defense, and the larger national security community.

In addition to its studies, SSI publishes special reports on topics of special or immediate interest. These include edited proceedings of conferences and topically oriented roundtables, expanded trip reports, and quick-reaction responses to senior Army leaders.

The Institute provides a valuable analytical capability within the Army to address strategic and other issues in support of Army participation in national security policy formulation.